# LOOK TO THE SKY

a companion to the documentary film

**BRETT CULP**

LOST POET
PRESS

*For the real-life superheroes who believe in tomorrow.*

*You continue to inspire hope in all of us.*

# CONTENTS

# INTRODUCTION

The cable news show was screaming in my face.

I was checking out of a hotel in Seattle, rushing to get to the airport. The TV was too loud as I stood in the lobby waiting for my ride to pull around. There was a 50-something guy sitting there watching it.

I sarcastically asked him, "How do things look today?"

He said, "Same as always… hopeless."

I wasn't inspired to ask a follow-up question.

I thought about what he said the entire flight home. I wondered how many other people feel this way. Have we lost hope? If so, how did we lose it? Can we get it back? And what *is* hope anyway?

These felt like important questions.

Back in 2013, I was ready to release a feature-length documentary film I had produced and directed called *Legends of the Knight.* The movie tells the stories of everyday people who were inspired to become heroes in their own lives or in the world because of their childhood love of Batman. (Yes, Batman.) The film is about the power of stories and the capacity all of us have to be superheroes.

Rather than pursuing the traditional path for indie films of festivals and mainstream distribution, I decided to launch a unique initiative. My team set up a distribution arrangement that allowed anyone to request a screening of *Legends of the Knight* in their local movie theater to support a charitable effort. The profits from that screening would then be donated to that charity. In concept, it was an opportunity for individuals and organizations to invite their communities to come together to celebrate heroic spirit, encourage local families, and support a charitable initiative.

I loved the idea, but it was risky. Because we were giving away the profits, there was no budget for marketing or management. It had taken three years to produce the film, and we were putting it in the hands of strangers. What if no one requested a screening? What if the requested showings sold no tickets? A

Hollywood agent I spoke to about the concept made it clear: if this idea flops, you will have no chance of getting the film on digital platforms like Netflix and Hulu.

I was anxious, but we did it. And people around the world responded in an incredible way. A year later, *Legends of the Knight* had screened in 110 cities around the world, raising $100,000 for charity. The stories of encouragement and community building that came from those screenings are inspiring and beautiful. I spent most of 2013 crying while reading social media posts with the hashtag #WEareBATMAN. And then the film was on Netflix for two years. My confidence in the goodness of people was sky-high.

After being immersed in this uplifting project, I was eager to start work on another documentary. While I had spent 12 encouraging months at charity screenings with kids of all ages dressed in superhero costumes, it seemed like many other people were experiencing the world in an altogether different way. Between the daily news and the constant conflict on social media, their lives were filled with dark stories. And while these stories seemed to be considered the "important news", I began to question if it was the only news worth talking about. I wanted to know how some people seem to be able to focus their attention on something other than darkness and tragedy.

A constant bombardment of negativity can create a dark vision of the world. It may appear that everything is a disaster, hate wins, and we are essentially powerless to do anything about it.

Surrounded by these stories, the finale of our lives can seem determined from the start:

"Same as always… hopeless."

\* \* \*

I've spent my career as a filmmaker sharing uplifting stories. In those cinematic journeys, the word "hope" is used often in interviews and discussions. It's a standard term in our vocabulary, often used in religion, politics, and relationships of all types. But I am surprised how few people can actually define hope in a sentence or two. I would encourage you to take a moment right now and see if you can do it in a satisfying way.

What is hope?

I wasn't totally sure myself.

*Look to the Sky* was my quest to understand hope. Filming in 18 cities in three countries, I captured the stories of young people whose lives demonstrate the superhero spirit. I interviewed experts in psychology, literature, art, and philosophy to go deeper. After exploring heroic storytelling through the mythology of Batman in *Legends of the Knight*, it felt natural to focus on the flip side of the same coin. Superman was the perfect cultural icon for discussing our struggles with positive ideals, identity, and light in the darkness.

In the end, the film expresses my heart about hope in 72 minutes. But there was so much more to say, so I poured it into these pages. My goal is to help you uncover some of the possibilities that you might believe are lost forever. Because that's what hope does- it gives you the courage to envision the universe, and yourself, in a new way. Then, hope gives you the strength to pursue change.

Ultimately, hope is an unstoppable force because it isn't

dependent on the circumstances of the moment or what has happened in the past. Hope isn't a reaction to what is occurring right now. It's a way of looking at every experience through the lens of possibility. You acknowledge what *is*, but then focus your thoughts and energy on what *could be*.

Hope doesn't make promises. It unlocks possibility. And it is that sense of potential that can allow you to move forward, even when the darkness seems overwhelming.

Although he may have been a wonderful human being, that guy in the lobby of the hotel was wrong about the nature of hope. Hope doesn't hinge on today's news stories, the posts you see on social media, or the sad story you will hear from a friend. It's beyond your mood or level of motivation in this moment.

Hope is a choice to believe that there is good ahead. It is a way of seeing the world that reveals its true breadth and beauty, its struggle and triumph, its despair and faith. Hope sees everything, and then chooses to move toward the light and the opportunity for positive change.

As you read the stories ahead, may they inspire you to

dream about what is possible in your own life. For within that moment of wonder is the essence of hope, and the beginning of the beautiful things ahead for you.

Let's seek the light, together.

*This Is the Universe You Live In*

# GABI

*The Impossible Happens*

What kind of world do we live in?

Some would tell you that we live in a world where good things go bad, where darkness seems to thrive, and where lasting positive change is just an illusion. These people live their lives reacting to the circumstances of life with very little belief that something good just might be around the next corner. And yet, others would tell you that we live in a world where bad things can be redeemed, where light can still overpower darkness, and where hope still lives. These people seem to have faith that however difficult their circumstances might get, there is a reason to anticipate a positive outcome.

So which group is right?

Which world do we live in?

Which world do YOU live in?

At some point, each of us defines what we believe is possible. Children are open to pretty much any idea: a large guy with presents can fit down a skinny chimney, mommies can do miracles, and a blanket tied around your neck means you can definitely fly.

Growing up tends to make you more realistic. You have painful experiences, read articles, watch the news, and become an expert on life. You recognize ideas that are silly or that won't work out based on what you have seen and known throughout your years on the planet. There's some wisdom in this view of the world, and it keeps you from walking out into traffic or jumping off a building with that blanket tied around your neck.

I brought many of these conceptions to my journey to create *Look to the Sky*. Production on this film allowed me to meet an incredible collection of young heroes, and it changed my definition of what is possible for the world and for myself. I realized that we aren't as locked into a narrow view of what can and will happen as I thought we were.

As you experience the film and read these stories in more

depth, you might be tempted to believe they are special cases. You may think these kids have abilities and qualities you lack. You might feel that their experiences would never happen for you. It's okay for you to see it that way. You don't need to feel bad about it or feel pressured to feel differently. You probably have some good reasons for feeling the way that you feel. However... I would be honored if you would stay with me for a bit on this journey. Maybe you will find something here that will be helpful.

The first story in *Look to the Sky* is about a young lady named Gabi. The third of four girls, Gabi grew up in a family of dancers. They're used to bumps, bruises, and growing pains, so when Gabi fell on her knee at the ice-skating rink, her mother wasn't concerned. She told her to ice and elevate it and that the pain would soon fade. It didn't. After a few weeks and a series of doctor appointments, they received the diagnosis. At nine years old, Gabi had osteosarcoma, a type of bone cancer, in her knee.

Gabi and her parents were devastated, and Gabi's first fear was how this would affect her dancing. They learned they would have to choose from three options of removing and treating the cancer. They could amputate the leg almost up to the hip and give her a prosthetic, but her active capabilities would be limited. They could attempt a limb salvage, which would remove the cancer from her knee, while trying to save as much of the joint and her leg as possible. This was the most appealing choice for Gabi and her parents until they learned it comes with the greatest chance of the cancer returning and that walking, much less dancing, might be severely hindered.

The third option was a procedure called rotationplasty. This surgery would remove her knee and reattach her leg from the mid-shin down to the middle of her thigh... backward. Instead of facing forward, her foot would face behind her. Her ankle and heel could bear her weight in a prosthetic leg and act as a knee. The rest of her foot would go down into the prosthetic to help it move. Essentially, her ankle would become her knee.

Gabi immediately dismissed rotationplasty because the idea of a backwards, abbreviated leg seemed so strange. And it looked weird. She soon learned, however, that rotationplasty was her best chance to be able to have the most mobility and to dance again. The heel would bear her weight in a prosthetic without the risk and pain that would come from a rod in straight amputation.

No one knew for certain if Gabi would be able to dance again. But, in her heart, she was open to what was possible. That sense of possibility was the foundation of her hope.

After receiving chemotherapy, Gabi underwent the rotationplasty procedure. Healing proved to be a long and involved process. Before she could consider dancing, she had to re-learn how to walk with this change in her anatomy. Gabi had to retrain her mind to make even the simplest motion in her leg. Everything was backwards, and it took time for her brain to send the correct signals to create the proper movement in her leg. She worked on the range of motion in her ankle that had been stationary in a cast. Then, once her bones had fused together, she worked on bearing her weight on the foot that now served as her knee.

I remember watching my children learn to walk. When you are small, it's an adventure to explore the world in a new way and stretch your abilities. Although you fall down often, there is an innocent resilience that allows you to get back up again and again. I have tried to imagine what it would be like to go through this experience, and then, years later, to do it all over again. To essentially start from the beginning, relearning how to keep balance and perfect the motion of the joints and muscles, would be a massive undertaking. As I've thought about Gabi's journey, I've recalled all the skills and talents I have developed over my lifetime that are so essential to my daily life. I have imagined how it would feel to lose one of them and then spend years rebuilding this ability from the beginning.

Maybe you've had to do this in your life. Maybe you know exactly how this feels. Gabi faced this battle, day after day, continuing to hold to the belief that one day she might also relearn how to dance. After a year, when she could walk without the assistance of parallel bars, the doctors told Gabi she could try dancing again.

At this point in her story, Gabi had already earned my respect and admiration. She had survived the realities of cancer and chemotherapy. She had braved the unusual procedure of the rotationplasty. She had dealt with the feelings of despair and fear and loss that come with a circumstance such as this. She had learned to walk again.

But that wasn't enough for Gabi. She believed in something more. And so with an inspiring depth of courage, Gabi chose to approach the dance floor once again.

Dancing is about grace, beauty, and balance. But Gabi's body wasn't balanced. One of her legs was shortened and her foot was backwards. While her friends were moving on to the more advanced dance classes, Gabi spent many, many months with the younger kids, figuring out how to make her new leg accomplish some of the most basic moves. In her heart, she was ready to move ahead, but for her body, everything was difficult.

Have you ever gone through a time where you worked hard and paid your dues, but then it all fell apart, and you had to start at the beginning again? Maybe it was a career, or a relationship, or an important project. It's hard sitting at the "little kids' table" knowing there is something beautiful and powerful in your soul, but you can't quite express it. Life begins to feel like a closed, constrictive place with little room for you and your dreams.

But this universe isn't constructed from darkness and despair. It is founded on hope.

To understand the full impact of Gabi's story, I had to learn a bit about dance. While Gabi eventually learned to dance jazz and tap again, ballet dancing proved the most difficult with the prosthetic leg. To advance in ballet, you must learn to dance "en pointe". The phrase refers to the tips of the dancer's toes. To dance en pointe means to straighten the foot and then to walk on the tips of the toes.

If you and I had been sitting together in one of Gabi's physical therapy sessions many years ago—when she was crying and stumbling—I suspect we wouldn't have spent much time discussing whether she would one day dance en pointe. Our conversation would have probably been much less grand and expansive. We would have felt bad about the pain and the disappointment and the injustice of it all.

And while we would have been thinking small, Gabi's heart was already en pointe. She was already living emotionally in another space. She was so far ahead of us because while we were stuck in the hurt of the moment, she had moved on to the possibility of what could be.

The video of Gabi dancing en pointe with a prosthetic leg went viral almost immediately upon release. She had asked the person who designed her leg to create a special pointe foot for ballet, and the footage of her dancing touched the hearts of millions of people all over the world. There's a raw emotional impact in seeing her dance. We are inspired by her bravery, effort, and commitment. But I think there's something even deeper at work within us. I believe we are seeing a glimpse of a more powerful truth about the entire universe.

Gabi forces each of us to ask this important question: If we live in a reality where a teenager can lose part of her leg, learn to walk all over again, and then gracefully dance ballet, then what might be possible for each of us? What power is hidden inside of us that we haven't seen yet? What could we create together that we have yet to imagine? What other impossibilities could actually happen around us and within us?

When I look at Gabi's story, I'm inspired to look at the world with an open spirit, remembering that we live in a universe built on possibility. Everything you know was once unknown. Everything you see was once unseen. Each spectacular flower was a seed. Each world-changing invention began as a crazy thought. The world is filled with bankrupted entrepreneurs who now run successful international businesses, drug addicts who are now loving fathers, and lost dogs who have somehow been found. And girls who dance on prosthetic legs.

"I didn't know if it was possible ... but I knew that if it *was* possible... she could do it." When I heard these words from Gabi's sister, I knew what gave this young dancer her superpower. It wasn't a belief in impossibility. It was a belief in *possibility*.

Gabi believed. And because Gabi believed, Gabi tried. Gabi worked through the pain of recovery and the reality of loss and the fear of the unknown because she believed that this good and beautiful and miraculous thing of becoming a dancer after losing a leg was *possible*. She believed that if she put the work in, her efforts would bring her the amazing victory that she dreamed of.

This story isn't an impossible story. This story is simply the tale of something good in the world colliding with something good in a young woman, and her courageous belief that this possible thing would become a reality in her life. She didn't need to have a road map for what it would look like to go from possibility to reality. She only needed the heroic belief that it would one day be real.

It is *possible* for good and incredible and miraculous things to happen.

It is *possible* that those good and incredible and miraculous things will happen to YOU.

And when those good and incredible and miraculous things offer themselves to you, the question becomes ... will you have the courage to believe in that *possibility*?

THIS is the universe you live in.

And believing this is the beginning of hope.

# RANDALL

*Real Change Can Happen*

We like to think that we know how things work. Even if our vision is that the world is ugly, cruel, and unfair, there is a strange comfort in believing *we understand it*. There's less disappointment when people let you down because you had already predicted it would happen. Failure is somehow less painful when you believe it was destined. Depression can even seem a little less desperate when you resign yourself to it.

But life is weird. The moment you put everything into an orderly system, something happens that forces you to reconfigure it. Just when you are certain that the world is a cold, dark place, a thin beam of light sneaks through a window you thought was tightly shut. And, just for a moment, you are forced to rearrange the reality in your head to account for it. Something is different.

Once in a while, these sorts of shifts in our understanding

allow us to begin to wonder how much positive change is actually possible.

In high school, all the odds seemed to be stacked against Randall Drayton. His mother moved him and his brother from home to home, staying with friends, often in dangerous settings. He never had a stable father figure in his life. He had multiple arrests starting in the 6$^{th}$ grade, and he was expelled from three schools for violent behavior. When his mother was arrested he set out on his own, sleeping on the couches of friends with no one to supervise him. No one fed him or bought him clothes. No one made sure he went to school, did his homework, or lived in any kind of healthy manner. Soon he fell into some petty criminal activity of his own.

Randall had been abandoned, and he responded with anger. When he felt like someone was disrespecting him, he started a fight. When he wasn't fighting, he spent his days walled up with a silent rage. His aggression attracted concern from teachers and administrators at his high school, and finally one teacher reached out to begin interacting with Randall and soon discovered that he was basically homeless. She set up an appointment for him to meet Vicki Sokolik from *Starting Right, Now*, an organization that focuses on helping homeless teenagers in Hillsborough County, Florida. They've helped many unaccompanied minors and teens at risk, such as Randall, and placed them in healthy, stable environments.

The first meeting with Vicki and Randall was difficult for both of them. Randall didn't trust another adult claiming to care and telling him what to do. All of the signs pointed to Randall being a hopeless case. He was too hardened, too afraid and angry. How could change happen here?

Do you know someone who you feel confident will never change? Is there something in your own heart that you wish were different, but you believe will always be stuck? Are there problems you see in the world or in your community that you think are beyond repair? If you can identify something in life you feel certain will not ever improve, then you can sense what it would have been like in the room with Randall and Vicki at that first meeting. The outcome of Randall's life seemed destined, and it wasn't positive.

This is the *essence of hopelessness* - to see the negative and become convinced there is no possibility of change. It's like watching a rerun of a game where you know your favorite team has already lost. It won't be different, and it cannot be different.

All of us seem to have spaces in our hearts where we believe the final chapter of the story has already been written. We may not be consciously aware of it, but deep down we are 100% convinced that meaningful, lasting change is impossible.

In the last chapter, we talked about embracing possibility and being willing to accept that amazing things are happening around us all the time. But this is the painful, personal spot where we often draw the line. We say, "Sure, the world is filled with incredible stories, but that's not me. The statistics are against me. Most people in my situation never change, and nothing gets better. This is life, and anyone who says otherwise is not in touch with reality."

If those sound like words you might think or say, I understand. I've been there.

However, in my career as a filmmaker I have sat behind the camera interviewing so many real-life superheroes who defied the statistics. People who were told their dreams were silly, that they would be just like their father, that they would never break free from the life they hated, and that nothing truly spectacular was

EVER going to happen to them. And yet, they have built an incredible reality for themselves, standing against all the overwhelming "evidence" that they couldn't do it. Every one of these heroes I have spoken with has something very interesting in common. Many have strong confidence, but not every success story is built on absolute self-assurance. Lots of incredible people have been filled with self-doubt and anxiety about their ability to pull off the change they've dreamed of.

I don't think the common thread is faith in one's self. The foundational belief of people who create transformation is their unshakable sense that *we live in a universe where real, lasting change is possible.* Not that they are necessarily gifted to understand or create all the positive shifts, but simply that the shifts are possible. And that possibility gives them the energy and courage to wake up every morning and add their contribution to the effort and movement of change. Before they ever set off on a heroic quest, they feel deep in their beings that things can be different. They believe that enormous shifts in our feelings, circumstances, relationships, finances, and identity happen every day. They know they were born into a changeable reality and they commit themselves to live in the flow of it. They choose to allow opportunity for growth and transformation to work in their lives. And they give the best of themselves to that movement.

So, when Randall and Vicki sat together in that first meeting years ago, it would have been easy for both of them to declare that the statistics were not in their favor, and part ways. Even in a program accustomed to working with troubled youth, some of Vicki's co-workers advised her not to enroll Randall. He seemed too hostile and volatile. But Vicki saw a spark in him. Deep down, she knew something about life that opened her heart to the opportunity for transformation. And she invited Randall to join her in that space.

Although his acceptance was half-hearted, and his wounds were deep, Randall chose to consider the possibility that things could be better. The process of change was extremely hard, but Randall stayed committed despite the fear, pain, and frustration he felt. He believed real, positive change could happen. That same belief encouraged those around him to stay the course and not give up. With time, Randall began responding to their help.

He fought through counseling, life coaching, and adapting to accountability and structure. His grades started improving, he flourished at work, and he took leadership and relationship courses. He also had a passion for football, and the program nurtured it. His coach became part of his support team.

Randall's hard work paid off when he graduated from high school and went on to play football in college. Vicki and the whole team of people who had invested in him got to celebrate with Randall in this amazing milestone accomplishment.

After everything Randall has been through, he sees himself differently. Success is now in front of him. He has a bright future because he dared to participate in a change of direction in his life. When I first met him, his face didn't speak of a hard past or the baggage of anger and distrust. His smile was warm and genuine— and contagious. I saw his belief in himself and his positivity about the future. Now, Randall can talk about his past without discouragement or regret, because he sees those chapters of his story as fuel to keep moving forward.

Today, if the world seems like a dark place, it might seem overwhelming to reimagine everything. You may feel stuck in circumstances you can't change. There may be places in your heart that feel trapped in a loop of endless pain and defeat. Perhaps you are experiencing tremendous pressure, believing you are responsible for engineering and executing all of the transformation that needs to happen in your own life and in your community.

*Hope invites you to release that weight.*

Don't allow these challenges to overwhelm you. Let your primary task be to simply *hold space*. Hold a space in your heart for the possibility that real, lasting change can occur. Maybe. Perhaps. Give the possibility some room to breathe.

Ponder the possible.

Consider that change can really happen.

With time, hope can make a home there.

*This Is Your Identity*

# MARGARET

*You Are Powerful To Create Change*

I strongly suspect that you have no idea how powerful you are.

Maybe you pull back from your dreams because you made a mistake in the past that has left you feeling fragile. Someone's negative words might have become a voice in your head that keeps you from boldly moving forward. Fear of change, failure, or criticism might be controlling you. Although you didn't do it intentionally, perhaps you have allowed yourself to be defined by boundaries that aren't real.

My friend Margaret might be able to help you see this differently. Before Margaret's eighth birthday, a postcard came for her father from The iF Foundation. This particular postcard was asking for donations for their Haitian Pride Breakfast outreach. The program provides breakfast sandwiches to school children across Northern Haiti. For most of the families, affording an education is such a strain that most of the children go without breakfast. Margaret thought of her own routine each morning. Breakfast was a given. She'd never considered that some children might have to go without it.

The thought of these children going hungry upset her. But what could a seven-year-old girl do? What did she have that could help?

When you are faced with an overwhelming problem in your own life or in the world around you, your abilities and resources usually appear small in comparison. You feel that you have so little, and solving the problem requires more talent, energy, and resources than you have available. Your financial debt keeps creeping up, but your income stays the same. You know your marriage is in trouble, but every attempt to fix it seems to make it worse. You allowed your academic GPA to get so low that even perfection in the upcoming semester seems like a waste of time. Sometimes, even if you hold that space for hope of change, it just doesn't appear that you possess anything to contribute to that change. The temptation is to declare victory impossible, believe you are a failure, and find a couple of nice shows on Netflix to binge.

There is both naiveté and beautiful simplicity in Margaret's reaction. She announced her intention to use her upcoming birthday as an opportunity to raise money for the Haitian Pride Breakfast outreach. Instead of presents, she would request that donations be made to the program in her name. At seven years old, she didn't have money or influence. But she realized that she had one asset: her birthday.

Think about Margaret for a moment. She must have considered what she would have to give up, and how that would feel at her upcoming party. Childhood birthdays are sort of a sacred thing, aren't they? They are an asset, not easily pried from a child who has experienced the pleasure of asking for all the things she wants, and then receiving those things. Birthday presents, in particular, are a kind of cultural birthright in America. Margaret decided to use that power, that leverage, as an opportunity to meet the needs of others. She decided to give what she had.

Her father arranged a meeting with Eileen Spencer from The iF Foundation. Margaret prepared for the meeting, writing down questions and then taking notes on their answers. She was fully committed to understanding the program, the need of the

Haitian school children, and exactly how she could make the biggest impact. With her parents' help, she set up a fundraising page through a website called Crowdrise. She then wrote the description for her page and sent the email out to friends and family along with the birthday party invitation. And those people began to share it. Soon complete strangers sought out her page to donate. Margaret received letters of encouragement from people she didn't know, who were inspired by her desire to make a difference. The total rose to nearly $4000, only to be doubled by an anonymous donor. With nothing more than a birthday, Margaret raised $8000 to provide breakfast to school children in Haiti! It was enough to feed a whole school breakfast for a year.

Her accomplishment inspired those around her. Her school invited her to speak about the foundation and how she had stepped outside of herself to help others. Her friends began repeating her efforts on their birthdays. Margaret did the same for her ninth birthday and plans to do it again for her tenth. Giving up her presents that one year became a movement that has made a difference in the lives of countless Haitian school children.

Early in the filming for *Look to the Sky*, I spent two days at Margaret's home in New Jersey. I interviewed her and her family about her birthday movement. In my mind, Margaret's portion of the film was complete after that. Then, that summer, I received a call from Eileen—Margaret wanted to travel to Haiti to meet the children her compassion had fed.

A few months later, I met Margaret at the airport. This would be Margaret's first flight out of the country, and she was optimistic. Still, I was concerned for her sensitive heart in traveling to Haiti. From my previous travels there, I knew how overwhelming it could be. Haiti is a beautiful country with beautiful people, but it can be a shock. The difference in cultural norms stirs a sense of danger, both imagined and real, and the lifestyle there lacks many of the comforts we know in the U.S.

As we walked out of the airport, people swarmed us— asking for money, asking for work, offering to carry our bags and wash our windows. We met our driver and began our travels down bumpy roads, past unfinished buildings, to a small village outside the city.

The nights were hot and loud and uncomfortable. We slept under mosquito nets in the humidity listening to dogs barking, people yelling, and the sound of passing mopeds. But Margaret never complained. Instead, she played with the kids and asked lots of questions. The local children would light up when the translator asked if they'd like to give Margaret a hug. They all played soccer together, made art, and taught each other little games. I saw the bond between Margaret and the Haitian children that she had first felt in her heart upon hearing of their poverty. Children see the world with simplicity and innocence.

When Margaret got to know these children she had helped - their joy and happiness, and their kindness to her - she received a gift that could never have been wrapped for a birthday party. The kids celebrated and embraced her. She felt loved and connected. And she knew that she had made a difference.

Margaret saw a need. Instead of turning away, distracting herself with her own life and the gifts she could have felt entitled to, she used her birthday as leverage to create change. That sort of sacrifice is at the core of any superhero story.

No matter where you find yourself today, *you have something*. A smile. A hug. A kind word. A birthday. And when you are willing to give it to a noble mission, magical things can happen. You find that you are powerful to create change in your own life and in the lives of others.

Many have trouble recognizing their power because they are too focused on their fears and limitations. When you focus on what's missing, you will always feel weak. But, if you embrace the idea that you are equipped to create change, then you allow that same possibility that flows throughout the universe to flow through you. Abilities surface. Opportunities present themselves. Like Margaret, you begin to see yourself as powerful.

Maybe you are feeling empty and struggling to find strength in any part of your life.

Maybe all you have is a birthday.

Maybe that is enough.

Margaret's story invites us to embrace the childlike belief that we each have the capacity to be the force behind change in ourselves and in the world.

# SANAH

*Being Yourself Is Your Superpower*

Since 1938, creators and fans have debated a deep philosophical question: Which is the real person - Clark Kent or Superman?

Some believe mild-mannered Clark is the real identity, with Superman as the costumed character he wears for daring adventures. Others see the moments in a Superman uniform as his truest self, and the reporter persona as the disguise.

Many superhero characters feel this tension within their stories. It's the struggle for identity. Who am I, really? How should I define myself? When I have the power to be anything, who am I supposed to be? These questions are significant, and they aren't simply for comic book heroes.

For me, this symbolizes the challenge we face when we look at our own lives. Heroes like Superman represent the growing sense of personal power we are experiencing as a global society. Certainly the world isn't perfect, but the average individual has more power to share their voice, create change, and do something impactful with their lives than the vast majority of humans who have lived in previous generations could ever imagine. We are realizing that we are powerful. And, like Superman, we are making decisions about who we want to be and what we will do with our newly-uncovered strengths. Our answers will all come down to what we believe about our *identity*.

This discussion about Superman's dual-identity kept playing through my mind as I spent a day filming with Sanah Jivani. By the seventh grade, Sanah had lost all of her hair due to alopecia, an autoimmune condition that causes the body to mistake hair follicles for invading cells. Sanah endured an amazing transformation while dealing with the effects of her condition. Now a senior in high school, she's shown the warm brilliance of her own true colors and inspired many to do the same.

I spent an entire school day with Sanah. I walked down fluorescent hallways amidst the clang of locker doors. I sat in the library that smelled of old paper, and I ate taco casserole while a crowd of voices echoed through the cafeteria. Memories of my own high school experience were triggered walking into the classrooms. I remembered the vulnerability, the social awkwardness, and the sense of urgency to find my place in the world.

I have always been a highly sensitive person. The blessing of this sensitivity is that I am more aware of everyday beauty. I quickly understand and connect with others. But the harder part is that rejection cuts more deeply, and unkind "jokes" don't roll off easily. I had some rough days in high school. As I recalled my challenging experiences, I imagined how it would feel for a young girl with no hair to walk down those halls. I tried to think about my teenage insecurities coming to life in her situation. Despite trying to feel powerful and secure in her world, she'd feel the stares and hear the whispers each time she passed a group of students.

Confidence was a long way off on that morning in seventh grade, when Sanah awoke to find the majority of her hair still lying on her pillow. In her family's Pakistani culture, long hair is a sign of beauty. Her mother would brag about Sanah's long, black locks with the unique gold streak that made her stand out as a child. The shedding of her hair felt like the shedding of her beauty, and Sanah was devastated.

Leaving the house with no hair was unthinkable. Sanah demanded a wig before going to school. She would tell her classmates that she'd had her hair straightened, and she thought no one would notice. She was wrong. Kids are smart, and they can be mean. At first, everyone stared, then began to talk behind her back, and finally began teasing her to her face.

Kids—and adults, if we're honest—do desperate things to fit in. We turn on each other for fear of being cast out ourselves. Sanah's classmates displayed a vast and deeply rooted fear. They pointed and laughed when she was around and left vicious hate notes on her locker when she wasn't. The most crushing blow came when they mentioned her wig on a social media "burn page", where students write cruel things about others. They robbed even her illusion of confidence.

Sanah tried to be brave, but inside, she hated herself. The teasing and bullying only confirmed how she already felt. As a result, she punished herself. She stopped eating for a time and began cutting her own body. Many find self-harm a difficult concept to understand. As Sanah describes it, when you hate yourself that much, you feel a release, like you're inflicting the punishment you deserve. I think that's why we sometimes feel drawn to hurt ourselves and each other. From the insecurity of bullying to the self-hatred of cutting, we make negative choices from a place of pain. We believe lies about ourselves, and that belief hurts, so we express the suffering we feel. It doesn't seem to make sense, but this is the strange logic of pain as it works within us.

In the summer before Sanah started high school, the pain became too much. She was alone. Each morning she felt like she was putting on a false identity. Her true self – her personality and passions – was fading from neglect. Sanah knew she had to leave her path of self-destruction.

She made a decision to live without her wig.

That decision determined her destiny.

She started small, taking her wig off for a few moments at a friend's house or the pool. The vulnerability was painful but also freeing. Sanah felt an immediate change. She started enjoying the things she used to love again and finding comfort in her friends. She saw that happiness was waiting where she'd left it. Her pain had only blinded her to it while she was lost in self-hatred. As she began to accept herself, she found hope again.

And she decided not to hide anymore.

Before the next school year began, she made a Facebook video to share the peace she had found. She talked about insecurities, and about the ways that people hide their true selves. She encouraged everyone to stop being afraid and to embrace who they are. In a powerful moment, she removed her wig on screen and said, "Sometimes you do feel like a freak, and you do feel like you don't fit in, but… I have one thing that no one else has, and I swear you have that too. You're *you*… And you should take that one thing that you have and *shine*."

Sanah had found her superpower. And people responded.

She noticed that after the initial shock, her peers at school seemed pulled toward her, with compassion rather than judgment. When she first lost her hair, she'd seen herself as ugly and incomplete. The kids at school picked up on it, feeling repelled by those feelings. Now, her positivity and self-compassion attracted people to her. When you love who you are, others are compelled to know you, to be in your space. There is something about a vulnerable, confident, kind-hearted person that invites those behaviors from others. I saw that phenomenon at her school. Teachers were inspired by her positive presence. Her friends had only praise for her influence in their lives. By choosing to be authentic, you attract authentic people. You find where you belong.

This kind of vulnerability frees you to give love. One way Sanah loves others is through Natural Day. She saw the pain and loneliness in those around her. Not everyone has alopecia, but anyone can suffer from anxiety, poor self-image, or personal traumas and fears. She knew the gift she had received was too precious to keep to herself, so she approached the principal at her school with the idea for a day to celebrate self-acceptance. He suggested that Sanah announce the day in front of everyone at a school assembly. In a move that would have been unthinkable a year before, Sanah stood up without her wig in front of all her high school classmates and told them how she had been freed from self-loathing and how they could be free too.

On February 13th, Natural Day was celebrated by the entire campus. Sanah chose the day before Valentine's Day to illustrate that we must love ourselves before we can effectively love others.

From Spring, Texas, the celebration of Natural Day grew to 17 schools in the U.S., then on to schools in France and the United Arab Emirates. Now it extends across 28 different countries through the hashtag, #NaturalDay, on social media. Everyone is encouraged to let go of that one thing that they are hiding behind. Some might decide to go without makeup or designer clothing. Others might open up about conditions or traumas they spend so much energy trying to conceal. People place sticky notes everywhere with positive messages like, "You're beautiful" for all to see. The effect of this simple gesture is so positive that school teachers leave the notes up long after the day is done. Online, people write posts and share pictures of themselves glowing with confidence. The goal is to inundate people with positivity, to build them up in a world where fear tempts us to hurl negativity instead. As a college student, Sanah is continuing to invest her efforts into Natural Day. She envisions it as a life-long mission to help young people embrace their beauty and share their unique gifts with the world.

So what about you?

If you choose to believe that you live in a universe where impossible things are possible, where real change happens, that's a beautiful beginning. Soon, you will discover that you are powerful to create that change. Then, like Sanah, you may just find that your power lies in places where you are most different. Your power lies in your unique identity in this world.

Being yourself is your superpower.

It's often much more comfortable to focus on what makes us the same as others. We were born to feel connected to each other, and we seek similarity as a way to build relationships. So we show everyone the normal, average parts of our heart and push down the stuff that makes us different. But our strengths are in the things that make us special.

Your greatest contribution to the world is probably waiting within the secret identity you are uncomfortable to share.

Each of us makes a choice about who we want to be. Many of us do it unconsciously, based on beliefs we inherit from family and friends about who we are supposed to be and where we fit in the world. Most of what we are told about ourselves is well-intentioned and meant to help us avoid pain. Unfortunately, it usually shows us how to be normal. And you can't save the world with normal.

Our lives are constructed around the identity we build. Decisions about relationships, careers, lifestyle, and ambitions all spring from the way we see ourselves. You have the power to accomplish extraordinary things, and you can overcome obstacles that seem impossible, but you cannot rise above your self-identity. You will never be more than what you see yourself to be.

You may have allowed your greatest strengths to become a secret identity. Perhaps you have lost yourself in an attempt to live up to something you thought you were supposed to be. Maybe that path has left you feeling lonely, afraid, and in despair.

Hope rests in knowing that you can shift that direction, and that your strength is not in some far-off place. You are carrying your superpower with you.

# KJ

*You Can Build Connection*

We know we live in a world of possibility. We realize that real change exists in the world. We believe that we as individuals are powerful to create that change and that our superpowers are already with us.

These are wonderful ideals, and I believe they are real. But sometimes the society around us seems to be telling a different story. It's easy to find examples that seem to disprove every line of this chapter's first paragraph. The narratives that can feel most troubling are those showing how we treat each other. Most of the unsettling headlines in our daily news could be summarized this way: "Someone did something to someone else, and it wasn't very nice." It is one story after another of people treating each other with disrespect, violence, and malice.

Some of us are drawn to these stories with the same urge we felt at school when someone yelled "Fight!" We run toward it because we like the drama.

Many of our favorite films are filled with conflict. Stories where everyone gets along for two hours aren't very exciting.

Imagine how boring sporting events would be if we stopped keeping score and there was no winner. Without the competition, it's just not interesting.

We like watching news programs and reality shows where people argue and have trouble getting along. The drama adds to the tension, engaging us to pick sides and to be invested in the outcome of the conflict.

Next time you find yourself frustrated at the negativity of our news programs, remember that the news is a business. They need to attract your attention so they can sell advertising spots. And they know you are drawn to stories where someone does something to someone else that's not very nice, so they tell those stories.

It can be good to be drawn to conflict. That instinct

motivates us to fight the battles and deal with the challenges we face in our personal lives every day. It inspires us to have the hard conversations and go through the messy situations of life. I think the problem happens when we become so overwhelmed by stories of trauma and viciousness that we believe this is the *norm*. We begin to feel that everything is unsafe and no one can be trusted. And, despite our ideals and dreams about the world, deep down we lose faith in humanity. In our hearts, the prevailing story is that humanity is wired for war, and we are destined to destroy each other.

I think that's why we need more kids like KJ.

KJ was nine-years-old when I met him, and he'd already written and published his first book. KJ's father is an author of children's books, so when KJ expressed an interest in writing, his father encouraged it. Soon KJ had come up with the idea for *Kacey's First Day of Basketball Practice*. KJ's uncle is deaf, and KJ wanted to help people understand more about the deaf community and about how people with differences should be treated.

The child in the book, Kacey, decides not to wear his

hearing aid at basketball practice. He's afraid of what the other children will think of him if they see the hearing aid and find out he has challenges with his hearing. Kacey's father helps him accept and be proud of who he is, and then to help others understand. The book even ends by teaching the reader a few basic words in American Sign Language.

What inspires me most about KJ is that he didn't consciously set out to bring people together. He writes from a childlike innocence. He wrote about basketball because he loves basketball (He beat me soundly on the court during filming!) He wrote a book about being different because his uncle is different. KJ knows what he loves and what is important to him. His book helps individuals come together to understand each other. It builds connection with people who might otherwise feel estranged or disconnected from each other. Instead of inviting conflict, it embraces connection and encourages relationship. Though written about Kacey, the book is for young people who aren't deaf. The goal of the story is to help kids understand and accept people who *are* deaf or who have challenges with their hearing. When you can acknowledge and accept the difference between you and someone wearing a hearing aid, then you can accept and understand people with different needs and journeys, different races and cultures. Real community becomes no longer a dream but a reality.

As a documentary filmmaker, I have captured stories around the world. I have attended charity screenings of my films in a wide variety of communities. I have spoken to audiences of thousands of people in large auditoriums, and we have shared hugs and tears afterward.

I know this for certain: *the world is filled with good people.*

There are so many people who want beautiful things for their own lives, for their families, and for the world. They aren't perfect, but deep down, I believe they are good.

Yes, the human heart has the capacity for destruction and hatred. The stories of conflict and violence come careening at us every day, and we are tempted to believe that this is who we are. But I believe our identity as a people is more accurately defined by compassion and beauty. I believe that as we look for places to connect with people who are a little different than ourselves, we will discover more and more of that compassion and beauty surrounding us.

We have work to do. But all of it is possible and changeable. And each of us is uniquely gifted and powerful to make it happen. When you believe we can connect, you create hope. It creates hope for you, for others, and for the world. You realize that everyone has a place. Everyone is needed and loved. We *can* work for hope by building community.

*This Is Our Struggle with the Darkness*

# THE DEGARMO FAMILY

*Your Greatest Strength is in Your Deepest Pain*

It's easy to give an inspiring speech atop a mountain of sunshine and flowers. It is much harder to speak those same words in a valley of shadows. Does this concept of hope and possibility actually hold up when everything really hurts?

Dan and Serena DeGarmo live in rural Chillicothe, Ohio. Dan is a minister and the entire family is active in their local church. In 2013, their family had 6 children.

On a day when everything seemed normal, Serena walked into the baby's room and found him lying still, with blood on the sheet next to his face. He wasn't breathing. She took his clothes off and watched his chest to be sure. There was no movement, so she began to perform infant CPR on her baby boy.

Between the breaths she breathed into Azaiah's tiny mouth, she shouted for Noah, her twelve-year-old son. He called 911, and then for his father. Serena knew Azaiah was gone, but the ambulance rushed them to the hospital in a desperate attempt to save the boy. It was not to be. When Dan arrived, he walked into the room where Azaiah's body was resting. As a minister, he had stood in this room before, comforting families that had lost a child. Now, it was his family. His child.

Losing a child is a devastating experience. The suffering for Dan and Serena was deep and painful. Throughout their grief, they noticed that while their community supported the two of them with calls and visits and care, most people didn't know how to provide support and care for their other five children who had lost their baby brother. They realized that the culture of comforting the bereaved often overlooks children who have lost their siblings. Noah, for example, suffered from anxiety after Azaiah's death. It affected his performance in school, and rather than consider that he had just lost his baby brother, the school accused him of being "dramatic".

Dan and Serena chose to bring their family in on the conversation, and the kids had a pretty amazing response. They felt strongly that something was missing for children who have lost a brother or sister, and they wanted to do something about it. They wanted other children in their shoes to know that they are not alone. They wanted to acknowledge this dark place of pain, and then to bring some light to it in a way that only a child can do. Noah, Ellie, Jada, Kiki, and Addie decided that they would put together care packages for other children who have lost a sibling.

Sometimes the DeGarmo kids take the care packages to funeral homes, showing up in a real, tangible way. They walk up to grieving children and say, "My brother died too". They form an instant bond. They don't need any formal words about feelings and loss. They just love each other, whether it's through hugs or playing together, showing those in pain that they are recognized and their pain is worthy of attention.

Each of the DeGarmo children places something different into the care packages they send out. They try to tailor it to the child in need, learning about likes and dislikes regarding toys and books. Then, Noah, Ellie, Kiki, Jada, and Addie each add their own personal touches to communicate love to the grieving child. Addie, for example, can't write yet, so she uses a marker to scribble on the outside of the box. When her father asks what the markings say, she answers that it reads, "God loves you".

Each package contains snacks, a stuffed animal or pillow to hug, tips the children learned on dealing with emotions that come with the loss, handwritten notes from the kids, and a large, painted rock. Azaiah's middle name was "Stone", so the children call these rocks Azaiah Stones. They write the name of the brother or sister who passed away on the rock.

On the surface, these kids don't seem to have superpowers. But they have the ability to look at someone else who has faced tragedy and say: "Me too. You're not alone. My story is like your story."

For me, their courage and willingness to look this darkness in the face is the best kind of heroic. These children will develop many strengths over the course of their lives. But their greatest strength, this strength of empathy, has been forged by the deepest pain they will ever experience.

I know people who are confident in their beliefs about the reason and meaning of these kinds of tragedies. They can tell you about the philosophical realities of suffering and explain the problem of pain with concise theories and bullet points. But after spending lots of time hearing the stories of people who are hurting, the answers are less clear to me. I don't know why bad things happen to good people. I do not have a simple explanation for the darkness that exists in the world and in our lives.

I'm not smart enough to know the WHY of suffering. But the beautiful people I have encountered as a filmmaker have given me a glimpse into WHAT we have the capacity to do when we experience it.

With a loss of this enormity, there must be times and spaces to grieve, cry, be angry, talk about feelings, and process the pain. For the DeGarmo family, this will probably always be part of their life experience on some level. That hurts. I wish no one ever had to live through that anguish. But, somewhere within all those wounds and heartache, they found a place where they could bless others.

Because of their painful experiences, these young people were able to support and care for others in a way that no one else could. They could identify with other kids in a way that adults, and even professionals, couldn't. They found themselves inspired and gifted to meet a need in the world.

Their pain became the source of their power.

So what do we do with our pain, then? What do we do with the darkness we face in our own lives, in our own hearts? What do you do with the broken parts of yourself that have never quite healed? Could it be that opening yourself to share your pain with others can be a catalyst toward healing and a place to find your greatest strength?

Now, this requires a kind of authenticity that leaves us feeling vulnerable. When we talk about our pain, we are venturing into the places where we are most raw and sensitive to the careless words of those who might misunderstand or belittle our struggles. This vulnerable feeling is totally valid and real, and it even protects us sometimes. It isn't typically safe for you or for others to go public with unprocessed pain without some help. But I have observed that being real about your difficulties and finding places where you can openly share your feelings is a big part of the healing process. There is no shortcut to bypass the hurt. You can't go around it, under it, or over it. You can only find strength by going through the pain.

I wish there were an easier way. Opening our hearts to process our pain is messy and hard and scary. But on the other side is a certain kind of peace for you, and a gift to share with others. The struggles you have experienced become a kind of unique "superpower" that can truly bring hope and healing to the lives of others.

Every story of inspiration and possibility, every heroic tale you've ever heard, includes pain. Our favorite stories aren't about characters who are having a wonderful day where everything goes perfectly. The most famous books and movies are about people going through a personal hell, or facing their worst fears, or risking everything. The stories we cherish are the ones with the biggest challenges, the biggest stakes, the biggest losses.

But we don't love these stories because we enjoy watching people suffer. We love them because in the best of the stories we are inspired by the *response* to the struggle and loss and pain. We see the best of humanity when we see a character rise after a fall, or fight after a failure, or love after a broken heart. We look at our own distress and we catch a glimpse of how it might *transform* us into something more. We may never really know the reason for the hurt, but we have the ability to uncover purpose within the pain.

I don't know exactly how to make sense of the tragedies you have experienced or will experience. But I am confident of this: *your greatest power to help others will come from the places where you hurt the most.* The heroic inner work you are doing as you fight through your daily battles is building your giftedness.

You will bless the world by looking into the eyes of others who have experienced the same pain and saying: "Me too".

# VIOLET

*There is So Much Light in You*

If we can learn to take the darkness in our world and turn it into light, then we can learn to find strength in our pain. But what about what is *inside* of us?

When Violet was six months old, her mother noticed a strange glow around her pupil. Her parents researched online and discovered the glow could either mean a cataract or a rare pediatric cancer called retinoblastoma. They took her to a doctor and prayed for the best, but the specialist immediately saw a large tumor in her left eye. Violet started chemotherapy at seven months old, and the cancer went into remission. Her parents were hopeful that the worst was past.

Upon further testing, doctors found that Violet has a small deletion on one of her chromosomes that causes mutation in every cell of her body. In short, *any* of her cells could become cancerous. Every few weeks she undergoes an extensive examination under anesthesia, where doctors search her whole body for cancer that could present itself at any time. When I met her, Violet had already been to 21 of these exams.

A child with this sort of diagnosis would have every right to feel afraid, or discouraged, or self-focused. Can you imagine how you would feel if a possible sickness lurked dormant inside of you, waiting to destroy you without warning? Instead of seeing the light inside of herself, Violet could easily be overcome with the darkness.

But there is something inside this little girl that is so bright, no disease could ever truly dim it.

Meeting Violet is an experience. She is a gentle whirlwind of compassion. She insisted on giving me a hug the moment I met her. She wanted to know everything about me and authentically shared everything about herself. At five-years-old, she hates naps, loves animals, laughs at any joke you tell, and believes it is her duty to offer you the last spoonful of ice cream. She is simply one of the most compelling children that I have ever met.

It isn't only her personality that lights the world around Violet. She and her family have made a conscious choice to spread compassion and hope. After meeting many other kids who have been through similar experiences with cancer and illness, Violet and her family were inspired to put together "Blessing Bundles" to deliver to these young people. The bundles include many of the child's favorite kinds of toys and games. The gifts are nice, but what I saw these struggling kids enjoy most was the connection Violet made with them. She was so in-the-moment with these new friends. She made them feel seen and cared for. Some of their parents told me that Violet's visit was the first time they had smiled in a long time.

The darkness you experience in the world *around* you can really impact what you believe about the world *inside* you. You see endless global-level stories of hatred, selfishness, and despair in the news and in your social media feed. On a smaller scale, you hear the stories of other people's personal weakness and failings from co-workers, at the gym, in the school hallway, on the playground. Sometimes it just feels like everyone is a mess, so you start to believe that you are a mess too.

It is beautiful to create communities and support groups where people can be vulnerable and share their strengths and weaknesses in a real way. The purpose of these groups is growth and positive change. I love that. It's also powerful to discuss the problems we see in the world with a mind to take action and create a positive impact. But when our discussions about the darkness are nothing more than talk, when we speak about it in a way that does nothing but spread despair, anxiety, and judgment, then it's hard to avoid feeling that humanity is so deeply broken we can't recover.

Usually both the speaker and listener of these negative narratives feel a temporary satisfaction after the story is told. We are proud of our wisdom to identify and label the darkness, and, for a moment, we feel good about the fact that the story isn't about ourselves. We have uncovered the darkness in another person or place. It's somewhere far away.

But there's a problem. The more we focus on the failings in others, the more energy we spend thinking about how ugly the world is, the more we sculpt the perspective we bring to our own identity. As much as we might think it's about "them", ultimately our hearts cannot really tell the difference. In financial terms, when you devalue the stock of the human brand, by necessity you are lowering the potential you see within yourself.

If the universe is broken, then you must be broken.

If the universe is a mess, then you must be a mess.

If the universe is dark, then you must have that darkness inside of you.

That's why Violet is so important. That's why I wanted you to meet her in *Look to the Sky*. I think we are touched by Violet because, deep down, we know there is something in her that lives in us, too. She is constantly struggling against something that threatens to swallow her whole, but the purity of her light is magnificent. We are a little broken too, but *this* is who we are. This light that we see in Violet feels so familiar because we have seen it someplace before - somewhere inside. And then we cry because we are afraid we have lost that part of ourselves. We worry that we will never feel that innocent and selfless again.

But what happens if we keep looking for the light? What happens when we keep our hearts open to see the places that compassion and hope still shine?

As a filmmaker, I am committed to telling uplifting stories. My mission is to lift up the light. My goal is to help those who hear and see these stories reposition their perspective on the world. I want them to be reminded of the truth that the world is filled with good people, that compassion is normal, and that our society is built not on laws and penalties but on an unspoken, public trust that we are actually pretty good at living out.

If we reframe the way we see the world, then we reframe the way we see ourselves.

If the broken can find healing, then you might find healing.

If there is beauty in the mess, then there could be beauty in you.

And if the darkness is always repelled by even the smallest amount of light, then maybe that small amount of light that burns inside you can actually make a difference. Even with all the challenges we face in our communities and within our own hearts, I believe we live in a benevolent universe. We struggle with the darkness, but love wins. The truth is that the light and love in Violet is also in you. You are both made of the same stuff.

I don't have all the answers for the challenges you are facing, but I know this for certain: *there is so much light in you.*

And that fills me with hope.

*This Is the Impact You Can Make*

# EMERY

*You Can Save People*

There's something about living with a spirit of hope that prepares you for an extraordinary destiny.

There's something about a belief in possibility that inspires courage and a willingness to risk. A sense of adventure and purpose and significance radiates from those who choose to fill their lives and hearts with the influence and the power of hope. A life such as this is always prepared and is always being *further* prepared to take powerful steps towards meaningful change.

Quite simply, hope equips you for the heroic.

Emery Benson was eleven years old when his family joined several others for a hiking trip in the Smoky Mountains. Ever the adventurer, Emery wandered downstream from the main group to explore. The rains had been heavy that summer and the river was deep and fast. Back at the top, seven-year-old Devin Leslie was standing on a boulder, moving too close to the edge of the river. Without warning, Devin's mom heard a splash. Her son had fallen into the raging current. He was struggling to keep his head above the water, and he was moving so fast she knew she would never reach him.

It was a desperate moment. Devin was in serious danger, and his mom was powerless to do anything about it. All she could do was scream, "HELP!"

A few hundred feet below, Emery was startled by her cry. He looked at the river and spotted Devin rushing toward him. In seconds, Devin would move past him and out of reach, and there was no one to assist in the river below. Emery had a split-second decision to make. Would he jump into the river in an attempt to save his friend?

It was very dangerous. It would be tough swimming for anyone, but it would be perilous for eleven-year-old Emery, especially in a rescue attempt for Devin. If he hesitated, Devin would be left alone in a life-threatening situation, completely out of control in the water. But if he jumped in, he was risking his own life and there would be no one to help. Emery's mother was upstream, too far away to advise him. He was on his own, and he only had moments to decide.

What would you do? Standing at the side of a violent river, hearing the cry for help, seeing your friend in peril, knowing you were the final lifeline, understanding the risk for yourself, and having no time to think?

If you were Emery's mother, and you were close enough for him to hear your voice, what would you shout to him?

These are exhilarating and rather terrifying questions, aren't they? A split second decision to take a risk—or to play it safe— could have cost either of the boys their lives.

Emery decided to take a leap. Without a moment of hesitation, he jumped into the water, swimming hard to reach the spot where he could intercept his friend. When Devin came toward him, Emery held him with one arm and used his other arm to paddle to the closest boulder. He pushed Devon up onto it and then held on for several minutes until the adults could reach them.

Emery made a daring move, certainly worthy of superhero status. When I asked him why he decided to jump into the river, he told me that he had just earned his swimming badge in Cub Scouts so he felt he could do it. I have no idea if having such a badge qualifies an eleven-year-old to jump into a raging river. I doubt it. But I'm touched by his belief that he could. He believed that he was powerful to save a life.

This was a scary, dark situation. Yet, Emery's instinctive reaction was: "I am ready, willing, and able to accomplish something heroic. Let's go."

I love that.

When we are willing to embrace hope, we are empowered to do bold, courageous things. That sense of possibility makes us brave. It inspires us to dive into new relationships, explore different opportunities, launch creative projects, and build innovative ventures. When you open yourself to the impossible, have faith in positive change, and see the light in yourself, you start to gain confidence that you can jump into the unknown and make an impact in your own life and in the community around you.

When the time comes to take a risk in your life, will you be ready to jump?

Here's my hunch: I think Emery's decision to take a leap was made *long before* that dire moment of decision. That choice was the result of years of encouragement and positive affirmation from parents and mentors. It was the build-up of a lifetime of experiences and perceptions. It was an expression of his identity that had been growing for eleven years. It was an expression of his view of the world and his place in it.

Maybe you are waiting for your big moment to shine and do something significant. Perhaps you are waiting for life to bring you an extraordinary chance to take an extraordinary risk. The reality is that *this* moment, even if it feels small and insignificant, is preparing you for the *big* moment. The choices you make when the spotlight is on you will be the result of the little choices you made when no one was looking. What you are investing in yourself and in other people right now is building your character and identity. Nothing is insignificant.

I spent two days filming with Emery and his family near Knoxville, Tennessee, where Emery enjoys hiking and camping and doing anything outdoors. I live in Florida. I grew up on comic books and video games, so for me, wading into a cold river in the Smoky Mountains with my camera was pushing the limits of my comfort zone.

On the first day, Emery led me an hour uphill to Mouse Creek Falls where the event had taken place. When we arrived at the spot Emery had jumped in, I set my backpack down on the rock to scout out the location. The rocks were slipperier than I'd expected, and after a misstep, I fell into the water myself! I still had my shoes on and my phone and wallet in my pocket. The current pushed me hard into a rock, leaving a huge, purple bruise on my side. I alternated between grabbing and slipping at the rocks for at least 20 seconds before making my way out. I pulled my phone from my wet pocket. It was dead.

My entire life is on my phone. It tells me where to go, how to get there, and who to meet. As I stared at the dark, lifeless screen, my heart sank. I felt stupid for making such an amateur mistake. I tried to stay focused on the shoot, but every five minutes I realized another consequence of my phone dying. I didn't remember my hotel name or how to get there. I didn't have my ticket info for my flight back. Maybe I could call my wife—oh wait… How was I going to survive?

Then, when I finally returned to my hotel that night and opened my laptop, I read multiple messages from friends about the passing of Lenny Robinson. Known as the Rt. 29 Batman, Lenny was the Good Samaritan I had featured in my previous film, *Legends of the Knight.* He drove his custom Batmobile to children's hospitals dressed as the Dark Knight himself to lift the spirits of those suffering. More than that, though, he was my friend.

Alone in my hotel room, there was no one to talk to. I couldn't send text messages or call anyone. The day had been overwhelming, and I still had to shoot the interviews the next morning. I questioned why I was even shooting this film. I felt weak and out of control.

It's fun when you are on the stage of a sold-out theater experiencing a standing ovation for a new film. It's nice when your movie debuts on Netflix and social media lights up with affirming posts about your work. But those beautiful moments happen because of the choices you make in lonely hotel rooms when your heart is broken and your phone is dead.

The next morning, I woke up and jumped into cold water

again. I was anxious, sad, and frustrated. But, deep in my heart, I trusted the journey. I believed I could find my power in the darkness. And I knew that I had the ability to make a positive impact. I didn't know if my new film would ever literally save a life, but I was confident that I could make a difference, even if it didn't feel that way on that particular day.

I think that's how hope works. It creates a foundation for the way you experience your life that allows you to keep moving on your noble mission even when things feel dangerous, out-of-control, lonely, and painful. Hope allows you to feel powerful, even when the circumstances are frightening. It gives you the courage to jump in and stay with the struggle when you are afraid. It motivates you to take action when the safer path is to stand on the riverbank and do nothing.

Hope is the impulse all of us need every day to keep fighting and to believe our work in the world matters. It's the strength we need to save a life.

# ANNALEISE

*You Have Something The World Needs*

You have something very special inside you.

I suspect you may have already discovered that I believe that about you. It's clear that I believe in hope and courage and light and that I believe you can discover those things in yourself. But there's something else inside of you, and I so deeply want you to see it.

This thing inside you is a gift. *Your gift.* It's something you bring to the world, something that fills you with joy whenever you do it. Maybe it's a talent or a skill. Maybe it's an interest or a dream. It's a passion that burns in you, at the core of your soul. It's the thing that makes you come alive.

You might know exactly what this thing is inside of you. Or maybe you have a vague idea of it that isn't defined. Or perhaps you have no idea what this gift is. That's okay. Every day is an opportunity to discover it.

But what do you *do* with this gift, once you have discovered it? Many of us discover our passions, only to decide that they aren't good enough or big enough or powerful enough to actually mean anything to anyone. And so we minimize these gifts inside of us, believing that they are not enough and we are not enough.

My intention is to challenge that kind of thinking. I happen to believe that you might just be able to reimagine that gift into something quite powerful.

At the age of fourteen, Annaleise became the youngest person to swim across Lake Ontario. For over twenty-six continuous hours, she persevered through tall waves and cold water, fighting her way across the lake and setting a world record. She did it to raise awareness and money for Camp Trillium, a place where children with cancer can go with their families to enjoy time together in a positive and encouraging environment.

Swimming 32 miles in open water without a break takes incredible resolve. But Annaleise's story began long before she entered Lake Ontario with crowds screaming her name. Her journey started a year before while visiting Camp Trillium with her swim team. Impressed by the courage she saw in the children who face the challenges of cancer, Annaleise wanted to help. She asked if she could volunteer but was told she'd have to wait five years to be old enough. She didn't want to wait – she wanted to help right away. A friend joked that in a few months she would be just old enough to attempt an open swim across Lake Ontario. To Annaleise, this crazy idea sounded perfect. If she couldn't volunteer to help the children at Camp Trillium, she'd just set a world record instead to raise money and awareness for the camp whose children had impressed her with their courage. And so she did.

When I heard about Annaleise's incredible achievement, I knew I had to meet her. This story went beyond finding hope or discovering identity or overcoming the darkness. It even went beyond leaving a positive, lasting change in the world. This story was about a young lady who *reimagined* her own skills and talents and passions into something the world needed. Her story needed to be told, not only because of the impact she made, but because of the permission it gives all of us to reimagine and embrace our own gifts.

And so, I set off for Canada to meet Annaleise. I was impressed by her quiet audacity. The idea of going out into the open water with the wind, the waves—and the eels—and swimming toward a destination so far away it can't be seen is beyond me. Not only was Annaleise the youngest person to swim across Lake Ontario, but she did so in weather that would have forced older and more experienced swimmers to give in and be pulled from the water.

When you think of a typical Olympic swimmer like Michael Phelps, there is a certain body type that comes to mind: tall, long arms, long legs, and long fingers. But Annaleise is tiny. Her strength is in her endurance. In competition, she isn't typically the first one to cross the finish line. Her superpower isn't swimming fast; it's that she never seems to stop. You might beat her in a sixty minute race, but I learned that she has unquantifiable powers that allow her to swim distances most of us couldn't imagine.

Something happened on my trip to Canada that helped me

understand just what Annaleise must have fought through when she swam across Lake Ontario to set the world record. On the first day of filming together, I arrived two hours early for a charity race. Annaleise was ready to swim, but soon the overcast sky turned to heavy rain. Someone announced that the race would be delayed. We all waited for one, two, and soon three hours.

Finally, officials announced that the weather was clearing and the race would start in two hours. That's when I realized there was an additional complication. For the swimmers' safety, the Coast Guard announced they wouldn't allow the swim to begin, even after the bad weather passed, until all boats in the area had been still for an hour. The closest dock for my boat was a mile and a half away from the race's starting point, and due to the water and wind from the storm, the boat would only be able to travel through the lake at five miles per hour. We did the math and realized we would need to leave in the boat that very instant to insure we arrived at the starting point in time to be immobile for one hour and not further delay the race. After three hours of waiting, it was then a mad dash to the boat!

In the still-pouring rain, I quickly boarded our zodiac, a small inflatable motorboat. As my assistant Braden drove, I sat uncovered in the rain, wind, and waves as we bobbed along. Although we were moving slowly, the waves bounced me around like crazy. My knuckles were white from gripping the side handles of the boat. As I sat freezing from the cold winds, I felt the opposing circumstances threatening my resolve.

Here I was in another country, stuck in a tiny boat, in a lake, in the rain. My phone had no reception, I was shivering, and growing seasick. And I'd yet to capture any footage of Annaleise in the lake. I fought to keep my equipment dry, trying to focus on thoughts of stillness to ease my stomach. It was a long two hours, and there was absolutely nothing I could do but sit, and wait, and stay hopeful. As hard as it is to accept, sometimes the uncomfortable place of waiting is exactly where you are supposed to be.

Then, at last, the race began. As though a switch had been flipped, the rain and wind stopped for twenty minutes. I captured all of the shots I needed.

When whatever struggle we are facing is over, our anxieties and discomforts seem almost silly. But in the moment of adversity, it would have been easy to allow fear to overtake me completely. It felt like everything was wrong. Tossed by the waves, I was literally and figuratively out of my element and had little control over my situation. You've probably felt that way before. It's natural to have a strong desire to be in control when circumstances make you uncomfortable. The ability to endure then becomes dependent on your faith and your focus.

Although I hadn't chosen the weather or the circumstances, I had made a clear decision to fly to Ontario and get in the boat on that rainy Sunday. There was a goal to fight for, much bigger than the waves splashing in my face. I believed in the film I was making and its ability to help people, and I was deeply motivated to continue the mission.

Swimming across Lake Ontario, I know Annaleise must have felt that same motivation for her own mission. She believed in the difference she could make for the children at Camp Trillium. She had reimagined her skills and passions into something that the world needed, but in the defining moments of the attempt, things got really hard. The challenges she faced in crossing that lake were immense, and Annaleise had to fight a huge mental battle. I tried to imagine what it would have been like for a 14-year-old to swim throughout the night, unable to see even a few feet ahead and wondering what creatures might be gliding just underneath her. She had trained as though the swim would take 15 hours, but because of the weather complications, it took her 26. If she focused on the darkness and the exhaustion, despair might have overwhelmed her. Instead, Annaleise focused on the goal she believed in and found strength to complete it.

When people ask Annaleise for advice on how to make a difference in the world, she always says, "Pick something you love, and never give up." She told me that she's always loved to swim. And she knows firsthand how good it feels to help people. So she found a way to do what she loves for the sake of those in need, and she inspires that selfless determination in others.

*She reimagined her passion into a superpower.*

You probably can't fly like Superman. And you may not be

able to swim like Annaleise. But you have other gifts, and you can choose how to use them. You can focus on increasing your power, wealth, and comfort, or you can make bold, world-changing decisions about how to use your gifts. You can choose a purpose that concentrates less on yourself and more on how your strengths can be used to help others. You can reimagine your passion into a superpower.

While making films like *Look to the Sky* and *Legends of the Knight*, I've connected with many different people and have learned valuable lessons about perspective. Those who spend their energy worrying and struggling only to meet their own needs tend to be unhappy. They live from a place of scarcity, thinking that the world contains only a limited amount of success and joy, and they have to fight others for their share of it.

You may find yourself identifying with that feeling, afraid that you don't have enough, constantly upset that others seem to have more. You may be working really hard to achieve more while constantly feeling exhausted and hollow. If you can relate to that emptiness, life probably seems unfair and frustrating. You are probably feeling powerless and weak.

The secret to abundance is shifting your focus toward using your gifts to help others.

In truth, a great endless lake of fulfillment exists. There is no scarcity. There is more than enough contentment and peace in the world for all of us to share, and people like Annaleise know how to dive into that lake and show others the way. Her success didn't come from focusing on herself and the stress of overcoming her own problems. Instead, she concentrated on the noble mission of making the world a better place, and her personal achievement flowed from that space of compassion. Without a focus on something bigger than herself, her record-breaking journey to swim Lake Ontario would have never even begun.

During the cold months leading up to her Lake Ontario swim, Annaleise sharpened her own superpowers at her local community pool. The pool is now named the Annaleise Carr Aquatic Center. As another example of her modesty in the midst of local celebrity, she works there part-time as a lifeguard. Though she was honored, she told me it's a little weird to work at a place named

after her. Nothing makes her happier than the difference she's made for the families at Camp Trillium. But in her heart, she sees herself as just another person with a gift, responsible for using it to make the world a better place.

We filmed at the Annaleise Carr Aquatic Center on Monday to capture some unique underwater footage. After the craziness of Sunday, I had forgotten my goggles. No problem, she said, and then showed me a large, overflowing bin of unclaimed goggles others had left behind. For me, it was another inescapable encounter with the abundance of good in the world. When you've done your best and appear to fall short, somehow, some way, help appears when you need it.

I was ready to film some underwater shots. I asked her to wait three seconds for me to get into place underwater and then swim above me while I filmed. Unfortunately, no matter what I tried, I couldn't stay on the bottom of the pool. As soon as I touched down I began to float back up. I felt silly telling Annaleise that I couldn't seem to stay down, but she told me the secret is to let some of the air out of your lungs slowly for as long as you want to

stay under. The exhaling of air keeps you from floating up. I was in no real danger in the lap pool, but it still felt a little scary. My lungs needed air, but in giving something up I thought I needed, I was able to capture something more permanent than a fleeting breath: amazing shots of Annaleise's form and technique from below.

By that point in the trip, I was starting to see my life like a slow exhalation of air. My instinct had been to hold as much in my lungs as I could, but I had to be willing to let go. As I sat on the bottom of the pool, gradually releasing the air from my body, while wearing borrowed goggles, I was feeling stronger. There was a voice in my head telling me it wasn't quite safe, but in my heart, I knew I was investing my gifts to make a positive impact for others.

On my final day of filming with Annaleise, we visited the camp for her annual swim with the kids she has helped. Each year, in the week that falls around Canada Day, the families at Camp Trillium swim across the camp's own Rainbow Lake. Children of different ages and medical conditions participate, and the event is part of what inspired Annaleise to take on Lake Ontario. Since that day, Annaleise has returned to Camp Trillium each year to swim

with the children and their families across Rainbow Lake.

When Annaleise experienced challenges and fears during her training to cross Lake Ontario, she thought about the stories of the young people who visit the camp each year. She realized that if they were able to face the trials of cancer each day, she could face the trials of Lake Ontario for what would turn out to be 26 hours, 34 minutes, and 11 seconds. In the process, she became an inspiration for the kids of Camp Trillium, who look to her record-setting swim for hope during their own struggles. The swim across Rainbow Lake is where they meet each year to celebrate and symbolically finish the journey together.

And she did finish with them. The swim took about 25 minutes, and Annaleise stayed in the water until everyone was out, moving around to different groups of people to speak with each swimmer. She encouraged them all to keep going and finish. She was talking about crossing Rainbow Lake, but I'm confident these heroic kids also took her words into their hearts for their difficult days ahead.

When you bring light into the world, it reflects in more

places than you can imagine. Annaleise has now completed multiple swims benefiting the camp. Although it is certainly possible to count the hundreds of thousands of dollars her swims have raised for them, the impact she has made on these young people and their families is incalculable. The smallest acts of kindness have power, even if you don't see it. A smile, a kind word, a hug, or a simple act of compassion can radiate and change someone's life in a way you can't predict and may never find out. Love is never wasted.

Annaleise has yet to meet her limitation as a distance swimmer. She's only been pulled from the water once, and it was because of adverse weather conditions. In all the vast distances she's swum, she has never reached the point of exhaustion or come to a moment where she can't continue. Knowing Annaleise, I suspect the depth of her reserve comes also from her belief in herself and the difference she longs to make in the world.

I have a feeling you haven't reached your limitations either. You might look around and say, "I'm not the fastest," or, "I'm not the most impressive." But deep down inside you there is the ability to keep going, to never give up until you have found your gift and a way to reimagine it into a superpower. You might hear a voice that tells you to stop, but I hope you will ignore it and press on to make your own difference in the world.

In 2012, a fourteen-year-old girl was told she was too young to volunteer at a camp for children with cancer. Instead of seeing it as rejection, it became the motivation to break records, help struggling families, and inspire countless people. What superpowers do you have? What good will come into the world from your struggle?

If we follow our passion and focus on something bigger, we'll find out just how high we can fly. Your gift can be your superpower. As Annaleise says, "Pick something you love, and never give up."

# SUPER EWAN

*You Can be a Symbol in the Never-ending Battle*

So, here's how HOPE begins:

You choose to experience life in a new way. Rather than seeing a small, narrow view of what is possible, you open yourself to a wider, more expansive perspective. You acknowledge that things that seem impossible happen regularly.

Then, within that framework of reality, you admit that maybe – just maybe – real change can happen. In a universe of possibility, things are constantly becoming different than they were. Over short and long time periods, major shifts are happening. And, if you can see it clearly in the world around you, then perhaps it can happen in the world inside you. Maybe lasting, meaningful change is possible. You begin to hold space for that movement.

As time passes, that hope takes root in you, and you discover that it has become a part of you. You begin to see possibility in yourself, possibility to create meaningful change. You even begin to realize the things that make you unique might actually make you powerful. As you become fully and powerfully yourself, you desire to connect with the world around you. You reach outside of yourself with compassion and empathy, and as you do, community begins to grow and change begins to happen.

Darkness will try and destroy the light you have discovered. But you won't allow it to extinguish that light, because you have learned that the power to truly connect is forged within the darkness. You will walk through the dark places, but you will walk with courage, because the hope at work in your heart reminds you that there is always light within you.

And so you will be brave. You will chase adventure and take risks. You will prepare for an extraordinary destiny. Perhaps you will even reimagine your deepest desires and gifts into something the world needs. You will find a depth of abundance in the face of scarcity, and you will discover that you truly do have superpowers after all.

And all of this… is only the beginning.

When I heard about the nine-year-old boy who wears a red cape to feed the homeless, I knew he had to be featured in *Look to the Sky*. I already had a few other stories about children feeding the hungry included in the film, so I wondered how he would fit. But as I got to know Ewan, I discovered something special. His heroic work had transcended his own efforts, and his story was about so much more than him.

When Ewan was six, his family drove from their middle-class suburb into downtown Detroit. They passed a homeless man on the side of the road, and Ewan began questioning his parents about the man's situation. He didn't like the answers he received and wanted to do something about it. His parents agreed. Soon they began handing out food and blankets to homeless people they would meet on the street. People found out about their efforts, and chose to participate and offer supplies and help. As donations came in, the family started driving into downtown Detroit every fourth Saturday to help as many people as they could. Ewan, his family, and volunteers set up grills and tables in Roosevelt Park and fed any who stopped by. They gave out nonperishable food items as well, along with toiletries, clothing and more. And all of it began with a child's desire to meet the needs around him.

He decided to wear a bright red cape on every outing. And people started calling him "Super Ewan".

Ewan and his family had been helping the homeless for three years when I met him. I'm sure he gets tired of doing it sometimes. After a full week of school, it's gotta be tough to give up Saturdays where you could be playing video games or sports. Many kids are distracted easily and tend to shift their interest in activities or pursuits. But Ewan told me about his long-term commitment to this project. It seems to be part of who he is.

Are there fewer homeless people on the streets now than when he started? He doesn't know. But he can tell you there are more smiles and more warmed hearts each time he goes to hand out hotdogs, socks, and toothbrushes. At first, that might seem naïve. But I think this kind of innocence that values relationship over results is probably exactly what this world needs.

Ewan calls the homeless community his "super friends". I tend to over-analyze things, and as I interacted with some of the people in Roosevelt Park, I wondered what to say and how to make them feel loved. But Ewan jumped into conversations with the same interest and respect he'd given me on our first meeting. He was very comfortable to hang out, chat, and learn more about them. He was never shocked by where they lived or the unique stories they shared. He was very curious about their lives. When one man arrived riding a bicycle he had cobbled together from spare parts, Ewan went up to him in awe. He began asking questions about the bike with the same fascination with which he'd looked over my expensive camera equipment. Super Ewan illustrated for me how we make people feel loved and respected by treating them no differently than we'd treat anyone else.

He wears the red cape, he says, so people will recognize his work and be inspired to help others themselves. And people *have* been inspired. Restaurant owner Chuck Speckman noticed the dedication and heart of Super Ewan and became one of his biggest supporters. Chuck is a success story himself, having overcome both drug addiction and homelessness. As a successful business owner, he couldn't help but be inspired to act and contribute when he saw Super Ewan's efforts. He believes that Ewan's greatest contribution to Detroit's homeless community isn't the handouts. It's the fullness in which the young boy gives his heart to those in need. He shows up month after month, wearing his cape and giving his time. People eat the food, and it's gone. They use the toiletries and throw them away. But people will always remember the time someone takes to show they care.

Chuck says that this kid is more than just a kid. He says Ewan has become a symbol in the community of compassion, service, and hope. His consistent choice to be there shows those down on their luck that they, too, can be more than what they are right now. They can break out of their cycle and embrace their own brighter tomorrows. And he's inspired others in the community to embrace their own charitable work.

Ewan's influence has reached beyond his city as well. I scheduled my filming time for *Look to the Sky* when I would be in the area speaking at the Hero Round Table Conference in Brighton, Michigan. Ewan was also a speaker at the event. He walked out on stage in his red cape and delivered his talk as easily as he'd chatted with people in Roosevelt Park while grilling hot dogs. His comfort comes from the genuine nature of his message.

See a need? Meet it.

Does it persist? Keep on meeting it.

I didn't get a standing ovation for my talk that day, but Super Ewan did.

I believe superhero stories are popular, now more than ever, because we are beginning to sense the superhero potential within us. Superman and all the superheroes that followed were created just ahead of major scientific and technological advances in Western Culture. Suddenly we could fly in planes and move from one place to another in a fraction of the time it took only a few decades before. We could erect tall buildings to the sky, and there were more advances just around the corner. Today, we can move, in a sense, faster than a speeding bullet via the internet. In a way, we're omnipresent, omniscient, and seemingly omnipotent. We have the power to reach and influence a vast audience with our words and behavior. We can hurt people deeply while remaining anonymous, with no seeming consequence. Or we can choose to bring comfort and encouragement. We can choose to bring light and hope.

I think we have become intrigued with the concept of the superhero because we realize that we have great power, and every day we are deciding how to use it. Stories about people with incredible abilities provide a way for us to look at ourselves and make those choices.

Super Ewan is a great kid doing wonderful things, but he has also become a symbol in his community. His work inspires people to ask themselves, "If this pure-hearted kid can show up month after month to help me and help others, what is possible for my life?"

In the moments of deep despair when you question yourself and the world, a young person like Ewan gives you hope. Against the pain that feels like it will never end, the losses that are breaking your heart, and the weakness you can't seem to overcome... hope wins. In the midst of the greatest darkness, hope is the enduring urge to rise up, keep moving, rebuild, and seek the light.

Super Ewan's hope inspires hope in others. Hope gives birth to hope. When you have hope in your heart, even if you have nothing else, you always have a way to change the world. I believe that's the greatest gift of seeing the world through the eyes of possibility.

Hope never ends with you.

Hope is always the beginning.

# CONCLUSION

*Encountering Hope in Cinematic Places*

Nine months into production on *Look to the Sky*, I had an emotional collapse. I experienced some personal losses that cut deeply, and I was really hurt. I felt so discouraged that I had to take an extended break from the project. I wasn't certain I would regain the energy to complete it.

As ironic as it might seem for someone making a film about hope to face such deep sadness, it made the process profoundly meaningful for me. I began this cinematic journey with a heart to share a positive message with *you*, but I chose to finish this journey for *myself*. I asked the questions I personally needed to answer, and I filmed with people who could speak the words I couldn't at that time.

In the editing room, I didn't want *Look to the Sky* to ignore the darkness in favor of the light. Every story in this movie shows heartache and sadness in an authentic way. Making this film reminded me that recovering the light often requires going straight into the darkness and choosing to shine within it. We can't avoid the darkness, but we can *transform* it.

I believe that the choices we make every day declare what we believe about the world and about ourselves. That's why it was important to me to finish the film. I want my life to shout "hope". And I want yours to shout it too.

Hope transcends every tragic story you've ever known. The existence of hope doesn't depend on what's going on in the world today. It isn't negated by your personal losses, as horrific as they might be. It isn't based on circumstances, or history, or international politics.

Hope isn't a logical reaction to what's going on around you. It's a firm belief that within everything there is positive possibility. It is cultivating a spirit to see the light in the darkness, in the world, and within yourself.

Hope gives you endurance in the face of doubt, fear, and failure because you believe something good is ahead. It allows you to stay focused on the important work in front of you because you believe it will lead to beauty, even if you can't see it right now.

When everything seems to be falling apart, hope still stands. When the circumstances tell you it's impossible, hope whispers a new idea. When you feel stuck, hope reminds you that your story isn't finished yet. When you feel powerless, hope reveals the impact of even the smallest movement. And when the darkness within and without feel overpowering, hope reminds you of your inextinguishable inner light.

Hope is unstoppable because it is anchored in a vision of both the universe and our own individual possibility that is beyond criticism, loss, setbacks, pain, adversity, and scarcity. How do you stop someone who is unaffected by these factors? Ultimately, you can't.

That's why I have fallen in love with hope, and why I believe that Superman is real.

I dream of a world where we spend our days looking to the sky.

I can't wait to fly with you there.

# REFLECTION QUESTIONS

**Gabi: The Impossible Happens**
- Have you ever had to go back and start from the beginning on a project or skill that was important to you?
- Have you ever witnessed something happen that seemed impossible?
- Is there something you desire for your life that feels impossible today?
- What would be different if that you believed that impossible thing was possible?

**Randall: Real Change Can Happen**
- What does "holding space for hope" mean to you?
- Despair is the feeling that things will never change. Is there something in your life that causes you to feel despair?
- If you believed change was possible in that situation, what change would you want to see?
- Is there space in your heart to believe that change could be possible?

**Margaret: You Are Powerful To Create Change**
- Have you ever witnessed a story like Margaret's, where someone creates powerful change in the world?
- Do you have a dream that you pull back from because of fear?
- What change would you make in the world if you knew you couldn't fail?
- What talents or resources do you possess that could create change for something or someone?

**Sanah: Being Yourself is Your Superpower**
- When you think about your own identity, what words come

to mind?

- What masks do you hide behind to make yourself more "ordinary"?
- What sort of person do you feel like you are "supposed" to be?
- What sort of person do you truly want to be?
- What unique characteristics do you have that you are afraid to let shine?
- What difference could you make in your family, your community, and your world if you allowed your uniqueness out into the open?

## KJ: You Can Build Connection

- Do you know someone who works to build connections with people who are different than themselves?
- Have you ever been a part of what felt like a true "community"? What was that like?
- Have you ever had an experience where your perspective on a specific group of people was changed because of a personal interaction with an individual?
- Is there a connection that you would like to build in your life right now?
- What community could you become a part of?

## The DeGarmo Family: Your Greatest Strength is in Your Deepest Pain

- Have you ever been changed for the better by hearing about someone else's pain?
- Do you have unprocessed pain that needs a space for healing?
- Do you have processed pain that you could share in order to benefit others? What would you share, and how would you share it?
- What would it look like for you to find your power in your pain?

## Violet: There is So Much Light In You

- What stories of goodness and hope have you encountered recently?
- Have you ever known someone who seems to radiate light, like Violet does?
- Do you believe you have that sort of light within yourself?
- What would change about the way you interact with the world if you did believe that that sort of light was within you?

## Emery: You Can Save People

- In what ways might you have been already prepared to be a hero?
- If you had been in Emery's position, would you have jumped into the river?
- Have you ever risked your personal safety to help someone?
- What decision could you make today that could save someone one day?

## Annaleise: You Have Something the World Needs

- What do you believe your gift is?
- Do you put your gift into practice on a consistent basis?
- Do you know anyone who has used their personal gifts to make a difference in the world?
- What would it look like to reimagine your gift into a superpower?

## Super Ewan: You Can Be A Symbol in the Never-ending Battle

- If you could be a symbol for anything, what would you want your life to symbolize?
- Is there a tangible need in your community or country or world that you have a desire to help meet?
- When you read Ewan's stories and the other stories in this book, in what ways are you most drawn to participate in

this movement of hope?
- If your hope could be the beginning of hope for someone else, who would it be?

# ACKNOWLEDGEMENTS

*My endless gratitude to:*

*Tricia, for dreaming with me & always believing in happy endings.*

*Logan & Judah, for helping me live heroically each day.*

*Mom & Dad, for showing me the stories worth telling.*

*Melody Farrell, for standing on the mountain with me.*

*Larry Green, for making me cry every time.*

*EVERYONE who contributed time, energy, talent, funds, and compassion to make Look to the Sky a reality. This happened because you helped. You continually remind me that the world is filled with real-life superheroes.*

*Thank You to:*

*Wilson & Becky Copeland, Southeast Psych, Michael Critzer, Dave Verhaagen, Jim Kwik, Ryan Hanson, Ken Kristoffersen, Chris Farrell, Bolaji Oyejide, Josh Costella, and Element.*

Through their not-for-profit organization *The Rising Heroes Project*, Brett and his wife Tricia produce inspiring films and create positive community initiatives. Learn more about their upcoming projects at: www.RisingHero.org

Follow Brett's adventures at: www.BrettCulp.com

CPSIA information can be obtained
at www.ICGtesting.com
Printed in the USA
BVHW061211110121
597454BV00004B/24